Bertie Travels

25¢

Written by Leta Potter
Illustrated by Maureen Fisher Rivkin

TUVWXYZ
TAXI CA

Bertie Bear went travelling.

May 5
Dear Friends,
I am in New York.
I saw a huge statue.
Love,
Bertie
25¢
Room 7
Park School
Paris, ON
N3B 1M2

He travelled by plane.

May 6
Dear Friends,
I am on a river.
I saw a huge alligator.
Love,
Bertie
Room 7
Park School
Paris, ON
N3B 1M2

He travelled by boat.

May 7
Dear Friends,
I am in the Rockies.
I saw a huge mountain.
Love,
Bertie
25¢
Room 7
Park School
Paris, ON
N3B 1M2

He travelled by train.

May 8
Dear Friends,
I am in the
Grand Canyon.
I saw a huge rock.
Love,
Bertie
Room 7
Park School
Paris, ON
N3B 1M2
25¢

He travelled by donkey.

LION HOUSE
Dear Friends,
May 9
I am at the zoo
in Toronto.
I saw a huge giraffe.
Love,
Bertie
Room 7
Park School
Paris, ON
N3B 1M2

He travelled by bus.

C D E F G H I J K L M N O

On May 10 Bertie was tired.
He went home to his friends